Original title:
Aligning Hearts

Copyright © 2024 Swan Charm
All rights reserved.

Author: Johan Kirsipuu
ISBN HARDBACK: 978-9916-89-028-8
ISBN PAPERBACK: 978-9916-89-029-5
ISBN EBOOK: 978-9916-89-030-1

A Serenade for Two

In twilight's glow we find our place,
Soft whispers dance, a sweet embrace.
A melody of hearts that sing,
In harmony, our souls take wing.

The stars above, a guiding light,
We share our dreams, the world feels right.
Each note we play, a gentle sway,
In love's own tune, we drift away.

In Tune with Our Essence

Beneath the moon, we blend as one,
A symphony that has begun.
With every laugh, a heartbeat shared,
In music's grasp, our spirits bared.

The rhythm flows like waves on shore,
A serenade forevermore.
Each touch ignites the sparks we feel,
In every note, our love is real.

Love's Intricate Weave

Threads of gold and silken dreams,
We stitch our hearts with timeless schemes.
In every glance, a tapestry,
Woven close, just you and me.

A dance of fate, two paths entwined,
In steps dance, our souls aligned.
With each embrace, our story grows,
In love's embrace, true beauty flows.

Threads of Destiny Interlaced

From distant shores, our fates entwined,
A journey shared, two lives aligned.
In every heartbeat, whispers soft,
Our destinies, forever loft.

We wander through this life as one,
In joy and pain, beneath the sun.
With every thread, our bond we weave,
In love's embrace, we dare believe.

A Symphony of Kindred Spirits

In whispers soft, our hearts align,
As shadows dance, our souls entwine.
With every note, a story told,
In harmony, our dreams unfold.

Through laughter shared, we find our way,
In twilight's glow, we'll laugh and play.
Together bound by threads unseen,
In this sweet song, we reign as queen.

Unwritten Melodies

Beneath the stars, a silence hums,
A tune unknown, as silence drums.
In beating hearts, the rhythm swells,
A world of dreams, where magic dwells.

With every step, a note we trace,
In swirling mists, we find our place.
The ink of night writes symphonies,
In every breeze, the sweetest keys.

Embraced Echoes

In hollow halls where echoes play,
We seek the light, we chase the day.
A laugh, a sigh, the stories weave,
In every breath, we learn to believe.

From whispered winds to distant chimes,
Each moment captured, lost in rhymes.
A gaze that lingers, a touch most true,
In fleeting time, we find what's due.

Beneath the Canopy of Stars

Under the vast and starlit sky,
We find our dreams as shadows fly.
With constellations as our guide,
In silent night, our hopes collide.

The moonlight spills on gentle streams,
While crickets play their softest themes.
In whispered prayers, we share our fears,
As time unfolds, we dry our tears.

The Language of Touch

Soft fingers brush against the skin,
Words unspoken, deep within.
A gentle hug, a warm embrace,
In silence, love finds its place.

A lingering glance, a fleeting feel,
Connections forged, raw and real.
In every caress, stories unfold,
A language richer than gold.

The Map of Shared Journeys

Two paths converge, a shared design,
Marking moments, yours and mine.
Through valleys low and mountains high,
Together, under the same sky.

Each step we take, a thread we weave,
In memories held, we believe.
With laughter bright, and joy in sight,
We navigate through day and night.

Synchrony of Two

Hearts aligned in perfect tune,
Dancing softly, like the moon.
In every glance, a symphony,
A duet made for you and me.

Breath by breath, we share the hour,
With every beat, we bloom like flower.
In rhythm's sway, we find our way,
Two souls as one, come what may.

Echoes in the Silence

In quiet moments, whispers play,
A gentle breeze, night turns to day.
Unseen shadows tell a tale,
Of distant dreams set forth to sail.

Within the hush, a heartbeat's call,
Echoes linger, rise and fall.
In absence loud, a love profound,
In silence, our souls are found.

Kinship in Cadence

In the whisper of the trees,
Laughter flows like gentle streams.
Hearts align in rhythmic beats,
Boundless joy in simple dreams.

Hands entwined under the stars,
Stories shared in quiet night.
A tapestry of soft touches,
Filling souls with warm delight.

Winds carry our secret songs,
Echoes dance through open fields.
Unity in every breath,
In this sacred space, love yields.

Each glance a spark ignites,
In harmony, we find our way.
Trust entwined, we rise as one,
Together facing dawn's bright ray.

Through life's labyrinth of days,
We find solace, hand in hand.
In every step, our spirits join,
In cadence, together we stand.

The Weaving of Intimacies

Threads of gold and silver spun,
Interwoven destinies glide.
Silent glances spark the fire,
In this warmth, our dreams reside.

Laughter weaves a sacred bond,
Memories crafted, softly sewn.
In each heartbeat, stories bloom,
In the tapestry, love is grown.

Fingers tracing ancient paths,
Mapping journeys, side by side.
In the loom of time, we share,
Every joy, through pain, we bide.

Whispers float on moonlit waves,
Secrets whispered, ever dear.
In the closeness of our hearts,
The fabric binds, we draw near.

Together stitching life's design,
Every moment, thread and seam.
In the embrace of tender ties,
Love creates our vibrant dream.

Together in Lyrical Motion

Dancing under skies of blue,
In the music, we find grace.
Every step a shared heartbeat,
In the rhythm, love's embrace.

Chasing shadows, laughing loud,
In every twirl, echoes soar.
A ballet of intertwined souls,
In harmony, we seek more.

With each note, the world fades,
Lost in melodies we make.
In the silence, sparks ignites,
Creating dreams that will not break.

Through the years, we move as one,
Every challenge, step we share.
In the cadence of our hearts,
Together, we breathe the air.

As the sun sets, we hold tight,
In this dance, we find our home.
With each heartbeat, side by side,
Together, we'll always roam.

The Canvas of Companionship

Brush of sunset paints the sky,
In hues that blend with softest light.
Every moment, strokes of love,
Together we create the sight.

Colors swirl in joyful dance,
Every shade a shared delight.
In the chaos, calm we find,
Creating solace, pure and bright.

Each canvas tells a story true,
In splashes, dreams and laughter flow.
With every tear, a richer hue,
In this art, our spirits grow.

We sketch the paths we've walked in time,
In vibrant strokes, our history.
Together crafting every line,
In our hearts, a mystery.

As the masterpiece unfolds wide,
With patience, love's colors blend.
In this artwork of our lives,
Companionship will never end.

The Journey of Synced Hearts

In the quiet dawn, we rise,
Hearts entwined, as sunlight flies.
Steps echo on the winding road,
Together, we share our heavy load.

Through valleys deep and mountains high,
Every tear turns into a sigh.
Yet in the shadows, love reflects,
A beacon bright, what life connects.

With each adventure, we draw near,
Facing storms, battling fear.
Within this dance, two spirits glide,
In the melody, love will abide.

As seasons change, we hold our ground,
In whispered dreams, our hopes are found.
Hands clasped tight, we chase the night,
Journeying forth, hearts burning bright.

No distance vast can pull apart,
The soulful ties that bond our heart.
In every breath, our tale unfolds,
A journey rich, our love retold.

Fragile Threads of Fate

In the tapestry of life, we weave,
Delicate threads that we believe.
Each moment strung with care and grace,
Paints a picture we can embrace.

When shadows loom and time stands still,
Our hearts connect, a sacred thrill.
Even in chaos, we find our way,
Guided by stars that never stray.

Whispers of fate, soft and clear,
Bond us close, nothing to fear.
In every twist, we find the strength,
To navigate love's vast length.

Through fragile ties, our spirits soar,
Braving storms, we still want more.
Each knot we tie strengthens the bond,
In every heartbeat, we respond.

Let time unfold what we can't see,
In every ending, a new decree.
United by fate's gentle tug,
In the shadows, we find our hug.

The Bond Beyond Time

In echoes of ages, we reside,
Where love's time bends and does not hide.
Across the cosmos, our souls convene,
In moments past, where dreams have been.

Time stands still when our eyes meet,
Moments captured, forever sweet.
Through lifetimes lived, we intertwine,
Writing stories forged in divine.

Though paths may diverge, love prevails,
With every heartbeat, it never fails.
Memories linger, shadows blend,
In the silence, we find our mend.

The ages may change but we remain,
In every joy and all the pain.
Infinite cycle, we restart,
Bound together, never apart.

So here's to the love that defies all time,
In every heartbeat, in every rhyme.
Through the fabric of existence, we roam,
Finding in each other, our eternal home.

Sways of Celestial Feelings

Beneath the sky, in twilight's glow,
The stars align, our love will flow.
Each flicker dances, a melody sweet,
Guiding our hearts, making us complete.

In the gentle sway of the night breeze,
We find ourselves, hearts at ease.
A cosmic waltz, so free and bright,
Wraps us close in its soft light.

With every pulse, the universe sings,
In shared laughter, eternity springs.
Through galaxies vast, our spirits rise,
Connected forever, no goodbyes.

As we journey through the celestial sphere,
Each whispered secret, cherished and dear.
In this ballet, no steps we miss,
Carried away on love's endless kiss.

So let the stardust guide our way,
In sways of feelings, come what may.
For in this dance, we find our souls,
Bound by the cosmos, forever whole.

When Souls Find Their Measure

In the silence, whispers grow,
Hearts entwined like roots below.
Time stands still in gentle grace,
Each moment etched, our sacred space.

Laughter mingles with the night,
Stars align with pure delight.
Two souls dance a timeless song,
Together where we both belong.

Through storms and skies, we journey forth,
Finding value in our worth.
In every trial, bonds are made,
Trust our compass, never swayed.

Eyes that speak a thousand dreams,
Reflecting light in silver beams.
With every heartbeat, love draws near,
In this embrace, we shed our fear.

And when we part, the echoes remain,
A melody of joy and pain.
In every corner of the heart,
Our story lives, we'll never part.

Cadence of Compassion

In every look, a silent prayer,
A gentle touch shows that we care.
Through thick and thin, we stand as one,
A dance of hearts beneath the sun.

With open arms, we meet the pain,
Sharing burdens like soft rain.
In kindness held, the world ignites,
Compassion blooms, our guiding lights.

Each heartbeat echoes, loud and clear,
A rhythm forged with love sincere.
Together we face the darkest night,
In harmony, we find the light.

When shadows cast a heavy pall,
Together, we will rise and fall.
With shared resolve, we build the way,
In unity, we find our sway.

Bound by threads of shared today,
We forge a path, come what may.
In every moment, love's embrace,
Cadence plays at a steady pace.

Embracing the Same Horizon

From different paths, we weave our fate,
Guided by stars, we anticipate.
With open minds, we journey wide,
Finding peace when hearts collide.

As dawn breaks o'er our shared domain,
Colors merge in a sweet refrain.
With every heartbeat, we align,
Seeking truth in every sign.

Across the miles, like rivers flow,
Into the depths, our spirits grow.
In every sunset, dreams ignite,
Together, we chase the fading light.

Through valleys deep, we climb the peaks,
In whispered hopes, our spirit speaks.
With every step, we nurture trust,
In this embrace, we both adjust.

And though the world may shift and sway,
The bond we share will guide the way.
Embracing all that lies ahead,
With open hearts, we forge instead.

Merging Pathways of the Heart

Two roads diverge in a gentle mist,
Yet in this choice, love's not missed.
With every turn, our fates entwine,
In every step, your hand in mine.

The path is long, the journey vast,
Yet echoes of our dreams hold fast.
In every challenge, we find strength,
Together we'll go any length.

As seasons change, we find our place,
In laughter shared, we call this grace.
With tender whispers in the dark,
In shadow or light, we leave our mark.

With every sunrise, hope is born,
In every dusk, we welcome dawn.
Two souls aligned in perfect tune,
Under the watch of the silver moon.

And though the ways may sometimes part,
Our spirits sing, a work of art.
Merging pathways, hearts afire,
Together we live our true desire.

Whispers of Sympathetic Souls

In the quietude of night, they speak,
Softly woven tales of the meek.
Hearts entwined in shared grace,
Finding solace in a familiar place.

Beneath the moon's gentle glow,
They share secrets only they know.
With every whisper, bonds grow tight,
Guided by love's radiant light.

Through trials faced and joy embraced,
Each moment savored, none misplaced.
In the tapestry of dreams they weave,
A bond so strong, none can deceive.

With every heartbeat's gentle sound,
In their union, peace is found.
In every struggle, they are whole,
The whispers echo, soothing the soul.

In twilight's hush, their spirits soar,
Understanding deeper than before.
As stars align in the vast expanse,
Together they weave a timeless dance.

Tuning to Each Other's Rhythms

In the symphony of hearts combined,
Every note a love well-defined.
A dance of souls in perfect time,
Melodies blending, a life sublime.

Through laughter's notes and sorrow's sighs,
They craft a tune that never dies.
With every heartbeat, they refine,
A harmony rich, truly divine.

In gentle pauses, they find their way,
Listening close to what words don't say.
Reverberations of love resound,
In their embrace, true solace found.

Together they navigate the storm,
Tuning each other, keeping warm.
In the rhythm of life's embrace,
They find their beat, their sacred space.

Each day a verse in life's sweet song,
In perfect harmony, they belong.
With every chord, their spirits rise,
Tuning to love under endless skies.

Dance of Kindred Spirits

In twilight's glow, they take the stage,
Hearts united, turning the page.
Each step a story, softly told,
In the warmth of arms, they behold.

Spinning freely, laughter in the air,
Every glance a promise, sincere care.
In sync they move, a gentle sway,
Guided by stars that light their way.

With every twirl, their spirits gleam,
A dance of love, a shared dream.
In the silent rhythm of the night,
Kindred souls, hearts take flight.

As shadows mingle, they intertwine,
Beneath the moon, their spirits shine.
Lost in each moment, spirits dance,
In the magic of love, they take a chance.

Together they weave the fabric tight,
In the dance of life, pure delight.
Every note a heartbeat shared,
In the dance of kindred, love declared.

Embracing the Echoes of Love

In the stillness, echoes resound,
Whispers of love all around.
Through the ages, they call and sing,
Embracing the joy that true love brings.

In the soft twilight, memories bloom,
Filling the heart, sweeping the gloom.
With every echo, a promise made,
In the tapestry of life's cascade.

Through the storms and sunlit days,
Their love endures in countless ways.
In every tear, in every laugh,
Echoes of love carve a lasting path.

As shadows whisper secrets deep,
In the arms of love, they gently leap.
Each embrace a testament to time,
In the echoes, their hearts chime.

With every heartbeat, they find their grace,
Embracing the love in life's embrace.
In echoes that linger like a sweet song,
Together forever, where they belong.

Fires of Shared Passion

In the glow of the night, we ignite,
Sparks fly high, pure delight.
Hearts entwined in joyful dance,
A symphony of fleeting chance.

With every laugh, the flames grow bright,
In warmth we find our shared light.
The world fades away, just we two,
A connection deep, forever true.

Through trials faced, we stand tall,
In the heat of love, we will not fall.
Fires rage, yet we remain,
Together bound, through joy and pain.

Whispers softly in the night's embrace,
Eternal flames, no time can erase.
Together we rise, never apart,
Forever lit, two beating hearts.

Our passion burns, a brilliant star,
In this life, no matter how far.
Through every storm, we find our way,
In the fires of love, we brightly stay.

The Connection's Fabric

Threads of gold woven tight,
In every laugh, in every sight.
A tapestry of tales we share,
Intertwined, in love's sweet care.

Moments dance like shadows cast,
In this fabric, memories amassed.
Each thread a story, bright and bold,
Together we weave, never old.

Stitch by stitch, through trials we stand,
Hand in hand, heart in hand.
The fabric stretches, yet holds strong,
In our embrace, we belong.

Patterns form in colors bright,
In every heartbeat, pure delight.
The connection's weave, a sacred art,
In this quilt, you're my heart.

Layers wrapped, we face the storm,
In unity, we're safe and warm.
Together we thrive, never to fray,
In this fabric of love, we stay.

Odes to Togetherness

In every heartbeat, love's refrain,
Together we dance, through joy and pain.
Odes we write in the stars above,
A melody of our endless love.

Hands held tight, we face the night,
Guided by the moon's soft light.
With every whisper, dreams take flight,
In this journey, all feels right.

Through winding paths, we find our way,
In sunlit fields, where children play.
Odes to moments, both big and small,
In togetherness, we have it all.

Each laughter shared, a gift so rare,
In the quiet, we find our prayer.
Bound as one, through thick and thin,
In this companionship, together we win.

With every sunset, our spirits soar,
In love's embrace, we seek for more.
Odes to us, in life's grand dance,
Together forever, in perfect chance.

Whispers Beneath the Stars

Underneath the cosmic glow,
We find the stories only we know.
Whispers soft like a gentle breeze,
In the night, our hearts find ease.

Stars align in perfect sync,
In their light, our spirits link.
Every twinkle holds a dream,
In this moment, love's sweet theme.

Through the silence, dreams take flight,
In the canvas of the starry night.
Words unspoken, yet understood,
In your gaze, I find my good.

Galaxies dance in the darkened sky,
In your embrace, I want to fly.
Whispers shared beneath the light,
Together, we define our night.

As constellations weave above,
In your arms, I find my love.
Here we are, forever blessed,
Beneath the stars, we find our rest.

Poetry of Mutual Dreams

In a garden where hopes reside,
Two hearts whisper, side by side.
Every thought, a soft caress,
In the glow of shared excess.

Winds of change gently sway,
Guiding dreams along the way.
Colors blend, creating light,
In the canvas of the night.

Each step forward, hand in hand,
Painting futures, bold and grand.
Silent songs in a soft breeze,
Words unspoken, yearning to please.

Together we weave the night,
Sparks igniting in shared flight.
With every laugh, the shadows fade,
In this union, we are made.

In twilight's glow, we embrace,
Finding joy in every space.
Together building, brick by brick,
In mutual dreams, we find our trick.

The Choreography of Unity

Underneath the starry dome,
We find our rhythm, find our home.
In every gesture, grace unfolds,
A dance of stories yet untold.

With every heartbeat, we align,
Steps uncharted, yet divine.
Through harmony, our voices blend,
In the swirl, we find a friend.

The world around may start to sway,
But in our steps, we find our way.
Each turn and twist, a silent vow,
In this dance, we live the now.

As shadows lengthen, we hold fast,
Creating moments meant to last.
In the silence, our spirits twirl,
A ballet woven, boy and girl.

Together moving, side by side,
In this rhythm, we take pride.
A choreography born of trust,
In unity, we rise robust.

Together in Rhythm

Every heartbeat sings a tune,
In the glow of the silver moon.
As we step, the world aligns,
In our laughter, the stars shine.

Through the silence, whispers flow,
In this dance, we learn and grow.
With every glance, our spirits soar,
In sweet harmony, we explore.

A gentle sway, a tender grip,
In this moment, we let it slip.
Holding on, yet feeling free,
In each note, our symphony.

Together we write, line by line,
A melody both yours and mine.
As dawn awakens, we see clear,
In this rhythm, always near.

With every step, our souls entwine,
In the music, we're divine.
Hand in hand, we chase the day,
In this rhythm, come what may.

Notes of Affection in Time

In an album of memories old,
We write every story bold.
Each note a line, a melody,
In the fabric of you and me.

Soft whispers linger in the air,
A sonnet crafted with such care.
Through seasons, love's gentle rhyme,
We find our way, transcending time.

With every smile, a chapter starts,
In this journey, we share our hearts.
Faded pictures, yet they shine,
In the echoes of the divine.

Each laugh a note, each tear a song,
In this harmony, we belong.
Together crafting soft refrains,
In the rhythm of love, no chains.

As the years weave through our days,
In affection, love finds its ways.
Notes of time play on repeat,
In this dance, our souls meet.

The Weaving of Tenderness

In the quiet loom of night,
Threads of kindness softly glow,
Woven hopes in gentle light,
Unraveling tales of love to show.

Hands entwined in soft embrace,
Stitching dreams with tender care,
Every touch a warm trace,
Whispers linger in the air.

Through the fabric, colors blend,
Past and future intertwine,
With each knot, new paths extend,
A tapestry, rich and fine.

Beneath the stars, we find our way,
Guided by the threads we share,
In this dance, we long to stay,
Crafting moments, pure and rare.

As dawn breaks with golden hue,
Our hearts, a canvas, bright and true,
In this weaving, love shines through,
A masterpiece made just for two.

A Journey Alongside

Step by step, we walk the road,
Side by side, through light and shade,
With every laughter, every load,
A bond of trust, together made.

Mountains high, and valleys low,
We face the storms, we seek the sun,
Navigating where wild winds blow,
In unity, we have begun.

The rivers sing a song for two,
Whispering secrets in the breeze,
With every wave, a dream anew,
Carved by time, through ancient trees.

Together, hearts and minds align,
Finding paths in tangled brush,
Each tender touch, a sacred sign,
In this journey, there's no rush.

As the sunset paints the sky,
We gather stars to light our nights,
With every glance, we wonder why,
This adventure feels so right.

When Hearts Reflect Light

In the silence of the night,
Hearts awaken, shining bright,
Mirrors of the soul's delight,
Reflecting dreams in silver light.

Every glance a gentle spark,
Illuminating all the dark,
In the warmth, no longer stark,
We find our way, a secret arc.

With laughter dancing in the air,
A symphony that we both share,
In this moment, free from care,
We paint our love, forever fair.

Caught in time's enchanting flight,
Together weaving day and night,
With every heartbeat, pure and right,
We become the stars' own light.

Captured in a tender glow,
In harmony, two lovers flow,
When hearts reflect, love's sweet show,
A timeless tale, forever grow.

A Culinary of Connexions

In the kitchen, flavors blend,
Chop and stir, let laughter mend,
Every taste, a note to send,
In this dance, we find our trend.

A simmering love, warm and true,
Spices shared, like dreams renewed,
Recipe of me and you,
Crafting memories, a delicious brew.

With every bite, stories unfold,
Gathering 'round, the young and old,
In each dish, a tale retold,
A feast of hearts, more precious than gold.

The table set with care and grace,
Smiles exchanged, a warm embrace,
In every scent, our roots we trace,
Together, in this sacred space.

As the candles gently glow,
And the evening starts to flow,
In this culinary show,
We savor love, let it grow.

The Surround of Silent Understanding

In twilight's glow, we softly tread,
Among the shadows, words unsaid.
A gaze exchanged, a heart's reply,
In silence deep, we learn to fly.

The world may buzz, but we remain,
Entwined in thoughts that soothe the pain.
No need for noise, our hearts converse,
In silent spaces, love's diverse.

With every breath, a rhythm grows,
A silent bond that ever flows.
In understanding's tender grasp,
We find our peace, as moments clasp.

Floating among the stars above,
Each twinkle speaks, a tale of love.
In silent waves, connections blend,
A timeless dance, no start, no end.

And so we walk, in quiet grace,
In this surround, we find our place.
With gentle whispers, hearts comply,
In silent understanding, we shall fly.

Harmony in the Whisper

Beneath the boughs, where shadows dwell,
The whispers weave a sacred spell.
In hushed tones, the secrets flow,
A melody that we both know.

The breeze carries our hearts' intent,
With every sigh, a truth is sent.
Together we hum a quiet tune,
In harmony under the moon.

Each rustling leaf sings soft and low,
Our laughter dances like the glow.
In every whisper, love's refrain,
An echo sweet, an endless chain.

With tender glances shared anew,
In every heart, a bond so true.
The night unfolds, our spirits rise,
In whispered dreams, our souls comprise.

Together we bask in this delight,
In harmony, we greet the night.
With gentle breaths, our love resounds,
In whispered tones, forever bound.

Unison of Echoes

In valleys deep, where echoes play,
Our voices meet, then drift away.
A soft refrain, a shared fate,
In unison, we resonate.

Each laugh, each cry, a sound so clear,
In every corner, you are near.
The world may fade, but we remain,
In echoes rich, love's sweet refrain.

Our words collide, a symphony,
In melodies, we find a key.
Through mountains high, through rivers low,
Our echoes dance, our spirits glow.

Though time may shift, and seasons change,
Our song stays strong, will not exchange.
With open hearts, we sing as one,
In echoes woven, never done.

Within the silence, we embrace,
In echoes shared, we find our place.
With every sound, our spirits rise,
In unison, we touch the skies.

Threads of Connection

In every thread that binds us tight,
A story spun in day and night.
Through laughter shared and tears we shed,
In every moment, love is spread.

The fabric of life, so richly sewn,
In every stitch, our lives are known.
Where paths entwine, we find our way,
In woven dreams, love's bright array.

Like colors bright, in harmony,
Each thread a part of you and me.
Together strong, yet softly worn,
In threads of connection, we are born.

We cherish the bonds that time bestows,
In gentle hands, the fabric grows.
A tapestry of hearts in tune,
In threaded smiles, we find our boon.

And as we weave our lives each day,
In threads of love, we shall not stray.
For in this weave, we are complete,
In connection's dance, our hearts repeat.

Symphonic Pulse

In the heart, a gentle beat,
Echoes through the night so sweet.
Strings of fate intertwine,
Creating music, pure, divine.

Soft whispers like the breeze,
Time sways with graceful ease.
Notes ascend and then they fall,
United, we find strength in all.

Harmony in every sigh,
Underneath the starry sky.
Rhythm guides us, hand in hand,
In this vast, enchanted land.

The pulse of worlds we share,
With every look, a silent prayer.
Symphony of souls aligned,
In this dance, our hearts entwined.

A crescendo, vibrant, bold,
Every story yet untold.
Together we will weave and play,
In love's symphonic ballet.

The Rhythm of Mutual Dreams

In the twilight, visions soar,
Together we unlock the door.
Dreams converge like rivers meet,
Flowing softly, pulse repeat.

Each glance, a promise softly spun,
In the silence, we have won.
Melodies of hopes aligned,
Beat by beat, our souls combined.

Walking paths of light and shade,
In the moment, fears do fade.
With whispers shared in moonlit glow,
The rhythm of love continues to grow.

Hand in hand, we chase the stars,
In every whisper, in every scar.
Threads of fate we gently sew,
Creating dreams that gently flow.

In our hearts, the music sways,
A dance of joy through endless days.
Together, we will find our way,
In the rhythm of dreams, we'll stay.

Tapestry of Affection

Threads of love in colors bright,
Woven tightly, day and night.
In every stitch, a story told,
A tapestry of warmth to hold.

Patterns formed in joy and tears,
Stitched with laughter, colored fears.
Crafting moments, rich and rare,
In each embrace, we linger there.

The fabric of our hearts entwined,
Patterns that fate has designed.
Underneath the gentle moon,
We weave our dreams, a sweet tune.

In the softness of your gaze,
I find the warmth that always stays.
With every touch, a thread anew,
A tapestry forever true.

Together, we create our space,
In this woven, sacred place.
Affection blooms, a cherished art,
In every thread, a beating heart.

Guiding Stars of Emotion

In the darkness, lights appear,
Guiding whispers that draw near.
Stars above, so bright and clear,
Mapping paths where we adhere.

Feelings dance like fireflies,
Flickering dreams under the skies.
Each heartbeat a gentle spark,
Illuminating love's sweet arc.

Through the night, we chase the glow,
Navigating the ebb and flow.
With each step, a heartbeat sings,
In the warmth that love can bring.

Stars of hope in twilight's embrace,
Crafting moments time can't erase.
As we journey, hand in hand,
Guiding lights across the land.

In the heavens, a dance divine,
Stars of emotion, yours and mine.
Together, we'll forever roam,
With guiding stars, we've found our home.

Unison in Longing

In the quiet night we stand,
Whispers softly filling the air.
Hands reaching out, warm and kind,
A dance of souls, a silent prayer.

Eyes that meet like stars ablaze,
Time suspended, hearts collide.
In the echo of gentle ways,
A bond that flows, cannot hide.

Dreams entwined like vines that climb,
Winding round through every heartbeat.
In this moment, frozen time,
Together lost, forever sweet.

Every sigh, a melody,
Every glance, a fleeting spark.
In the hush, we sway and see,
Our longing bathed in the dark.

Forever in this sacred space,
Where longing meets the tender light.
In unison, we find our grace,
Two hearts that dance into the night.

A Symphony of Understanding

In the orchestra of life we play,
Each note a truth, a gentle sound.
Listening close, we find our way,
In the harmony, we are bound.

Every laugh, a bright refrain,
Every tear, a quiet pause.
In our hearts, we share the pain,
Together strong, we find the cause.

Melodies of thoughts align,
In the silence, we perceive.
With each chord, our spirits shine,
In every word, we truly believe.

Understanding blooms like spring,
In the warmth of heartfelt grace.
Each conversation a sweet fling,
In the rhythm, we find our place.

In the symphony of shared dreams,
Echoes linger, soft and bright.
Together we create the themes,
A tapestry woven in light.

Hearts Entwined in Stillness

In the stillness of the dawn,
Where whispers linger on the breeze.
Hearts entwined, a gentle yawn,
Finding peace in shared hearts' ease.

Time slows down, a sweet embrace,
Two souls drawn in quiet tide.
In this sacred, calm-filled space,
We lay our burdens down and bide.

Silence speaks of love profound,
In every breath, a pulse of trust.
Roots of connection, deeply found,
In the stillness, we are just.

Moments drift like drifting leaves,
Softly tangled 'neath the sky.
In the quiet, love believes,
As time slips forth with every sigh.

In hearts' stillness, hope will rise,
A gentle glow that lights the way.
Guiding us through darkened skies,
Until the dawn of brighter day.

The Art of Resonant Hearts

In every beat, a story flows,
An art of love that paints our days.
Resonance in the highs and lows,
In quiet moments, always stays.

Every smile, a brushstroke bright,
Each touch, a whisper of the soul.
In harmony, we find our light,
Together we become more whole.

The rhythm of our lives entwined,
Like melodies that softly blend.
In the chaos, love defined,
An echo that will never end.

With every laugh, the canvas glows,
In every tear, a depth reveals.
The art of hearts, it gently shows,
The beauty in the way it feels.

In this dance of give and take,
Resonance becomes our guide.
With every choice that we do make,
The art of love will not divide.

The Pulse of Mutual Dreams

In the hush of twilight's glow,
Whispers of hope begin to flow.
Two hearts beat with a soft refrain,
In the distance, they share the pain.

With every wish cast to the night,
Together they seek a guiding light.
In the silence, their dreams entwined,
A symphony of souls aligned.

Through the shadows, they walk as one,
Chasing the warmth of the morning sun.
Every step brings them closer still,
In unity, they find their will.

Through valleys deep and mountains high,
Their dreams take flight, they learn to fly.
In the realm where hope is king,
Together they rise, their spirits sing.

In the dance of futures yet to weave,
They find the strength to believe.
In the pulse of mutual dreams,
Love is the force, or so it seems.

Navigating the Same Stars

Under the vast and starry dome,
Two souls wander, far from home.
Charting paths with stardust maps,
They navigate through gentle laps.

With every star, a promise made,
Guiding light that won't soon fade.
In the night, their whispers soar,
Connected hearts that yearn for more.

Constellations woven in dreams,
In every sparkle, their love redeems.
They follow the trails of ancient light,
Together strong, through darkest night.

When clouds obscure the shining skies,
They find solace in each other's eyes.
Hand in hand, they brave the storm,
In love's embrace, they keep warm.

Navigating tides of fate and chance,
They spin a web of sweet romance.
In the cosmos, their journey glows,
Forever bound, as time bestows.

A Tapestry of Shared Moments

Threads of laughter, woven tight,
Each moment glimmers, pure delight.
Stories shared under the sun,
In each chapter, two become one.

Quiet mornings, coffee's steam,
In simple life, they find the dream.
Every glance, a secret to hold,
In the warmth, their hearts unfold.

Time dances softly, gentle sway,
Painting colors in shades of gray.
Through ups and downs, they hold the thread,
In the tapestry of love, they're wed.

Each heartbeat stitches, every sigh,
In the fabric of life, they fly.
With every stitch, a memory sown,
A masterpiece created, love has grown.

In the twilight's glow, they find their place,
A tapestry woven with pure grace.
In shared moments, forever twined,
A story of love beautifully designed.

The Dance of Fated Connections

Underneath the silver moon,
Two destinies hum a tune.
They twirl in a cosmic embrace,
In this dance, they find their space.

With every beat, a spark ignites,
Binding hearts on starry nights.
Together they sway, lost in the song,
Fated connections, forever strong.

Through cycles of chance, they spin and glide,
In the whirl of life, side by side.
With every step, they weave a dream,
In perfect rhythm, they softly beam.

Their laughter echoes through the air,
In unison, they find their care.
A symphony of souls entwined,
In the dance of fate, love is blind.

As dawn approaches, the music fades,
Yet in their hearts, the melody stays.
Through every dance, together they'll roam,
In the pulse of fate, they find their home.

Interlace of Intentions

In a tapestry of thoughts, we weave,
Threads of hope and dreams we believe.
Hidden paths and shadows blend,
Each step forward, an unbroken trend.

With whispered wishes, we unite,
Casting visions in the fading night.
Laughter dances on the breeze,
Bonding hearts with gentle ease.

Through tangled roots, our spirits grow,
In the garden where intentions flow.
A symphony of voices strong,
Together we'll sing our lasting song.

Every glance a silent vow,
A promise made to the here and now.
In this union, we find our grace,
A sacred bond time can't erase.

As dawn breaks wide, our colors shine,
In harmony, our lives align.
With every heartbeat's rhythmic tie,
We trace our dreams across the sky.

The Pulse Beneath Serenity

In still waters, a heartbeat hums,
A quiet strength that softly comes.
Beneath the calm, a secret stream,
Woven life in a gentle dream.

Within the hush, a vibrant beat,
Resilient energy beneath our feet.
Echoes of laughter, whispers shared,
A silent bond that felt prepared.

Through shadows deep, where soft light plays,
The pulse of life within us stays.
Anchored hearts, we rise and sway,
In unison, we greet the day.

From tranquil shores, our spirits soar,
In the pulse, we find the core.
Where peace meets passion, there we stand,
Together, we become the land.

With every breath, we intertwine,
Serenity's pulse, a love divine.
In this embrace, we hear the call,
To dance through life, we'll have it all.

Wandering in Tandem

Two paths converge, a fateful meet,
In every step, a shared heartbeat.
With open arms, we brave the night,
Wandering souls, we find our light.

Through forests deep and mountains wide,
Hand in hand, we choose to glide.
In every laugh, a memory's trace,
In every challenge, we find our place.

The stars above, our guiding map,
In dreams we weave, there's no gap.
With every sunrise, a new dawn breaks,
Together we birth the love that wakes.

In the breath of wind, we dance and sway,
Faith and friendship lead the way.
As seasons change, our spirits grow,
In tandem, we learn what love can show.

Through every storm, we hold on tight,
In tender moments, we find the light.
Wandering together, our hearts aligned,
In this journey, true peace we find.

The Light of Shared Dreams

In flickering flames, our hopes ignite,
Casting shadows that dance in the night.
The dreams we weave, like threads of gold,
In the warmth of our hearts, a story told.

In whispered secrets, we plant the seeds,
Nurtured by love, fulfilling our needs.
With open eyes, we see the way,
Together we rise, come what may.

Each sunrise dawns with a palette bright,
Colors of passion, future in sight.
In the canvas of life, we boldly draw,
A masterpiece born from a shared awe.

Through valleys low and mountains steep,
In unity's embrace, our visions leap.
Hand in hand, we face the streams,
Guided by the light of our shared dreams.

As starlit skies unfold above,
In every story, we find our love.
With every heartbeat, we make a mark,
In the tapestry of time, we spark.

Waves of Affection

In the embrace of the sea's warm sway,
Gentle whispers dance on the bay.
Hearts align with each ebb and flow,
Love's rhythmic pulse begins to grow.

Tides pull close, then drift apart,
Yet still they bind each tender heart.
Moments rise like foam on the crest,
In waves of joy, we find our rest.

Every splash tells a tale of grace,
A journey shared in this vast space.
With every surge, a memory we weave,
In currents deep, we dare to believe.

The sun dips low, painting skies aglow,
As laughter mingles with the undertow.
Hand in hand, we chase the light,
In waves of affection, we take flight.

As the night unfolds, cool and serene,
Love in the moonlight's gentle sheen.
In tides of dreams, we closely bind,
Waves of affection, timeless and kind.

The Ties that Bind

In laughter's echo, true bonds are made,
Through every trial, love won't fade.
Hands held tight, through thick and thin,
Together we rise, a dance to begin.

The roots of friendship dig down deep,
In shared secrets, promises we keep.
Through storms and sunshine, we stand tall,
With the ties that bind, we'll never fall.

Each thread of memory, woven with care,
In quiet moments, our hearts lay bare.
We celebrate joy, we face our fears,
In laughter and whispers, throughout the years.

Distance may try to tear us apart,
But love perseveres, a steadfast heart.
In the tapestry of life, we find our way,
The ties that bind grow stronger each day.

So let's weave our stories, rich and bright,
In the fabric of friendship, day and night.
Together forever, no end in sight,
In the ties that bind, we find our light.

Confluence of Spirits

Two rivers meet in a sacred place,
Flowing together with gentle grace.
In the dance of souls, we intertwine,
A confluence of spirits, both yours and mine.

Hearts like currents, strong and free,
Winding paths toward destiny.
In the depths, our dreams collide,
In this merging tide, we abide.

With every whisper, a story unfolds,
In shimmering waters, our love beholds.
Boundless horizons, where we explore,
In the confluence of spirits, we crave more.

The ripples spread, a serene delight,
As we lose ourselves beneath the moonlight.
In the harmony of voices, we sing,
A timeless bond, a lasting spring.

Together we thrive, like rivers unite,
In the radiant glow of love's pure light.
With open hearts, we find our way,
In this confluence, forever we stay.

The Garden of Quiet Kinship

In a secret garden, where silence reigns,
Whispers of friendship flow in soft veins.
Petals of laughter, dew-kissed and bright,
The essence of kinship, a true delight.

Beneath the old willow, stories are shared,
In this sacred space, all hearts are bared.
Roots intertwine, deep in the ground,
In the garden's embrace, love is found.

Gentle blossoms, each fragrant and rare,
Nurtured with kindness, sown with care.
In twilight's glow, we watch the stars,
In the garden of kinship, fate leaves no scars.

Time flows softly, like a quiet stream,
In this haven of dreams, we dare to dream.
With every season, our bond will grow,
In the garden of kinship, hearts overflow.

So let us wander, hand in hand,
Among the blooms of this cherished land.
In the garden's embrace, we forever stay,
In the quiet of kinship, come what may.

Echoes of Shared Solitude

In whispers soft, we share the night,
Beneath the stars, a gentle light.
The silence speaks, a bond so pure,
In solitude's embrace, we endure.

Moments pass, like shadows fade,
In quiet spaces, love is made.
A heartbeat's echo, soft and sweet,
In solitude, our hearts still meet.

Breath by breath, we find our way,
In silence, words begin to sway.
Together here, we'll make our stand,
In shared quiet, hand in hand.

From distant dreams, our visions blend,
In solitude, we are a friend.
Like gentle waves upon the shore,
Our echoes linger, evermore.

As dawn breaks through the night's cool air,
The whispers fade, yet we still care.
In echoes lost, our spirits soar,
In shared solitude, we seek for more.

The Bridge of Warmth and Trust

Across the divide, we place our hands,
A bridge we build on gentle sands.
Each step we take, so softly tread,
In warmth and trust, our fears are shed.

The distance fades, as souls align,
In every glance, our hearts combine.
With laughter shared, and stories told,
We weave a bond, a thread of gold.

The sun may set, the night may call,
But on this bridge, we shall not fall.
In shadows deep, we find our glow,
In warmth and trust, our spirits flow.

With every heartbeat, we discern,
The lessons learned, the tides that turn.
Together strong, we rise above,
This bridge we walk was built on love.

When storms arise, we'll hold on tight,
In trust, we find the strength to fight.
Together here, we'll brave the gusts,
On this bridge, it's love we trust.

Heartbeats in Harmony

In rhythm soft, our heartbeats blend,
Each pulse a note, a song to send.
With whispered dreams, our spirits dance,
In harmony, we take a chance.

The melody of night surrounds,
In whispered breaths, pure love abounds.
With every laugh, a symphony,
In heartbeats shared, we both are free.

When shadows fall, and silence reigns,
Our harmony eases all the pains.
Together close, in time we find,
The beat of love, forever kind.

In every glance, a spark ignites,
Our hearts compose in starry nights.
With every touch, we feel the flow,
In harmony, our love will grow.

Forever tuned, our souls will sing,
In perfect pitch, with joy we bring.
Connected deep, we rise above,
In heartbeats shared, we find our love.

In Step with Affection

As sunbeams break through morning haze,
We walk together, in gentle ways.
With every step, our hearts align,
In affection's dance, your hand in mine.

The world around, a vibrant show,
In step with you, my spirit flows.
With laughter shared, our joys ignite,
In affection's glow, we find the light.

Through winding paths, and open skies,
In every glance, a soft surprise.
Together here, our worries cease,
In step with love, we find our peace.

With every challenge, side by side,
In affection's trust, we take the ride.
No fear can break this bond so strong,
In step with you, where I belong.

With every heartbeat, our journey grows,
In steps of love, the beauty shows.
Together always, our souls will dance,
In step with affection, we take a chance.

Serene Interlude of Love

In twilight's gentle weave, we find,
Soft whispers of the heart entwined.
In every glance, a world unfolds,
As passion's truth silently holds.

Tides of warmth in silence grow,
Each moment shared begins to flow.
Two souls adrift, yet anchored near,
In sacred spaces, love sincere.

Like autumn leaves on quiet streams,
We drift through life with tender dreams.
Our laughter echoes in the night,
A soothing balm, love's purest light.

In the stillness, secrets bloom,
Creating beauty from the gloom.
We dance beneath the silver skies,
In every heartbeat, love replies.

With every breath, a promise made,
In the soft embrace where fears do fade.
Together here, we craft our song,
In serene moments, we belong.

Where Minds Converge

In quiet corners, thoughts collide,
Two minds converge where dreams reside.
Ideas spark like stars in flight,
Creating worlds of pure delight.

Through gentle chats and laughter shared,
Each secret thought laid bare and paired.
Connections thrive in honest ways,
In shared pursuits, our minds ablaze.

With every word, a bridge we build,
A tapestry of heart fulfilled.
Together weaving threads so fine,
In this rich fabric, our lives intertwine.

Through silence, too, we understand,
The language of the heart is grand.
Without a sound, our spirits dance,
In perfect harmony, a chance.

In unity, we rise above,
Where minds converge, we find our love.
In whispered hopes and dreams we chase,
Together bound in time and space.

The Melody of Union

In every note, our hearts align,
A symphony of love divine.
Together crafting sounds so sweet,
In perfect time, our souls complete.

The rhythm pulses through the air,
A song composed with tender care.
Like gentle waves that kiss the shore,
Each harmony, we long for more.

With every word, a cherished tune,
The night transforms beneath the moon.
As melodies of laughter ring,
In every moment, love will sing.

Through crescendos and the soft sighs,
Our hearts will soar, our spirits rise.
With every echo, we'll endure,
A timeless bond, forever pure.

In the music, our dreams take flight,
In melodies, we find our light.
Through life's orchestra, we will roam,
In love's sweet symphony, our home.

Celestial Dances

Beneath the stars, we twirl and glide,
In cosmic waves, our hearts abide.
With rhythms known to hearts alone,
We dance in spaces, light as bone.

As planets spin with grace and flair,
We move through galaxies, aware.
With every step, the universe sighs,
In twinkling lights, our spirits rise.

A waltz of dreams through night's expanse,
In stardust trails, we take our chance.
With hands entwined, we whisk away,
To realms where love will always stay.

Each moment shared, a comet's flight,
In woven paths, we find our light.
The cosmos hums as we embrace,
In celestial rhythms, time and space.

Together bound by fate's design,
Two souls aflame, in dusk's decline.
With every heartbeat, we advance,
In endless love, our eternal dance.

Perfectly Synced

In the dance of night, we sway,
Underneath the moon's soft ray.
Two hearts beat as one sublime,
Lost in love, we traverse time.

Whispers echo in the breeze,
Gentle moments put us at ease.
Every glance, a tale untold,
In our arms, the world feels gold.

With every step, we find the way,
Two souls woven in this ballet.
Steps aligned, a rhythm true,
In every twirl, I'm drawn to you.

Through shadows deep and light's embrace,
Hand in hand, we find our space.
Tides may rise, storms may come,
Yet together, we are home.

Embracing day with endless grace,
In your eyes, my sacred place.
Perfectly synced, no flaw to trace,
In love's warmth, we find our pace.

Harmonious Heartstrings

In quiet nights, our laughter rings,
A symphony that love's heart brings.
Strings of affection softly play,
Guiding us through night and day.

Each heartbeat a note, warm and bright,
Creating melodies in the night.
Together we weave a song so sweet,
In every pulse, our souls meet.

With whispers shared, our secrets blend,
In harmony, our hearts transcend.
Every moment, a verse in tune,
Dancing softly beneath the moon.

The world may fade, but we remain,
Bound by love, free from pain.
Strings unbroken, forever tight,
Two hearts entwined, a wondrous sight.

Emotions rise like waves at sea,
In perfect harmony, just you and me.
With every breath, our song anew,
The heartbeat of love, forever true.

The Language of Connected Beats

When silence speaks, we understand,
A language spoken, hand in hand.
Each heartbeat whispers soft and clear,
In the stillness, I feel you near.

The rhythm flows like rivers wide,
In perfect sync, we take the ride.
With every glance, a thousand words,
In this silence, love's truth emerges.

Together we ebb, together we flow,
In quiet moments, love will grow.
Connected beats through night and day,
In the dance of life, we find our way.

Every heartbeat shares a thought,
In this language, love is taught.
No need for words, it's understood,
In every pulse, it's pure and good.

With gentle grace, we find our tune,
Under the stars, beneath the moon.
Connected beats, forever spun,
In love's embrace, we are as one.

Threads of Affection Interwoven

In the tapestry of life, we weave,
Threads of love, we gladly conceive.
Colorful stories blend and sway,
Interwoven, they light our way.

With every thread, a memory sewn,
In the fabric of time, our love has grown.
Soft whispers dance like threads of gold,
Binding our hearts, a tale retold.

Emotions twine like vines that climb,
Together we flourish, transcending time.
Every stitch a promise to keep,
In this quilt of love, dreams run deep.

Through storms and sunshine, we remain,
The strength of love, a sweet refrain.
In every knot, our hopes reside,
Threads of affection, side by side.

Together, we craft a masterpiece,
With every thread, our joy's increase.
Interwoven hearts, forever strong,
In this tapestry, we belong.

A Chorus of Soulful Yearnings

In the quiet of the night, we plead,
Whispers dance through shadows' weave.
Hearts entwined in a tender need,
Echoes of dreams that never leave.

Stars above, our hopes take flight,
Guiding us through the dark and blue.
In the silence, we seek the light,
An endless path where love is true.

Voices blend in a quiet song,
Carrying wishes on gentle choirs.
In this space, we all belong,
Finding warmth in the shared fires.

Threads of fate weave tight and close,
Each heartbeat sings a melody.
In the tapestry of souls that rose,
We find our strength in harmony.

Time may fade, but feelings grow,
Roots entwined like ancient trees.
In our hearts, a steady glow,
A chorus of soul that's meant to please.

Mirrors of Parallel Paths

Reflecting back in twilight's gaze,
Two souls walking, side by side.
In every step, a silent praise,
Journeying through fate's grand tide.

Winding roads beneath our feet,
Veils of time lay softly down.
In echoes of the past we meet,
Lessons learned in shadows' frown.

Side by side with hearts ablaze,
Sharing moments of joy and pain.
In the twilight, the world displays,
Mirrored paths in love's domain.

Beneath the stars, we wander free,
Two reflections of a single soul.
In this dance of destiny,
Together we become quite whole.

So let the winds of fate align,
Two kindred spirits, one heartbeat.
In every glance, our lives combine,
Mirrors shining where souls meet.

Serendipitous Harmonies

In the chance of light we find,
Melodies that brave the storm.
Whispers play in breezes blind,
Notes of life create warm form.

In the crowd, your smile appears,
Unfolding laughter like sweet song.
Moments shared melt away fears,
In serendipity, we belong.

Stars align in perfect spree,
Cosmic rhythms entwined, anew.
Every glance, a tune to see,
In this dance, love's promise grew.

Raindrops fall like gentle chimes,
Each drop playing its own part.
Nature's symphony softly climbs,
Crafting magic in the heart.

Together weaving dreams and time,
Unexpected moments intertwine.
In our souls, the sweetest rhyme,
Serendipitous harmonies align.

The Breath of Affection

In the softest sigh, a spark ignites,
Thermal whispers fill the air.
Moments shared in tender nights,
Every heartbeat laid out bare.

Fingers brush like summer winds,
Each touch becomes a sacred tune.
In the light, our love rescinds,
Shadows fade beneath the moon.

The world outside may drift away,
In our haven, time stands still.
Every glance, a dance we play,
In this warmth, we seek to thrill.

Breath by breath, we weave our tale,
A tapestry of love's pure bliss.
With each heartbeat, we set sail,
In the ocean of a timeless kiss.

So here within this gentle space,
Our souls entwined, we come alive.
In every moment, every grace,
The breath of affection will thrive.

Celestial Embrace

Stars entwined in the night sky,
Whispers of love softly drift by.
Moonlight dances on your face,
In this gentle, celestial embrace.

Galaxies spin, a cosmic waltz,
In your gaze, my heart exalts.
Infinite wonders above us play,
Guiding our souls along the way.

In the hush of twilight's kiss,
Time stands still, a perfect bliss.
Planets orbit, a timeless grace,
Bound together in this space.

Meteor showers paint the night,
Each flicker brings our dreams to light.
Boundless skies, a canvas wide,
Together, here, we will abide.

As dawn breaks, the stars retreat,
Yet in my heart, your love's complete.
Though the heavens take their leave,
In this embrace, I believe.

The Art of Synchronization

Two hearts beat in perfect time,
Rhythm of love, a lovely chime.
Every glance, a silent song,
In this dance, we both belong.

Hands entwined, our fingers weave,
In dreams, we dare to believe.
A cadence shared, just you and I,
The world fades as we fly high.

Moments blend, a seamless flow,
Like rivers merging, we will grow.
In the echoes of your laughter,
I find a joy ever after.

Steps aligned on life's grand stage,
Together we turn the page.
In each heartbeat, a story told,
Melodies sweet against the cold.

Graceful we go, like leaves in air,
Finding solace, a love so rare.
In this journey, side by side,
The art of life, our love as guide.

Hearts in Tandem

Two hearts racing, side by side,
In this rhythm, we confide.
Through every challenge, we will run,
Chasing dreams, our race begun.

With each heartbeat, we align,
A bond that only you can find.
In sync, our spirits soar,
Together, we can conquer more.

Like rivers flowing, wild and free,
In tandem, you belong with me.
Every laugh, every tear shared,
In this journey, we declared.

Through tempests fierce and skies so clear,
Our hearts whisper, 'I'm always near.'
In twilight's glow, we find our peace,
Together as one, our joys increase.

So let our hearts run, hand in hand,
On this soft and golden sand.
In this race where love's the key,
Forever together, you and me.

Convergence of Devotion

In the quiet of devotion's bliss,
Two souls meet with a gentle kiss.
Promises spoken, hearts laid bare,
In this sacred space, we share.

Tides of love wash over us,
In this bond, we place our trust.
Eternal vows, a solemn grace,
In every heartbeat, love's embrace.

Paths have wandered, yet we unite,
A convergence in the soft twilight.
Hands held tightly, we forge ahead,
With love as our guide, no fear of dread.

In the tapestry of fate we weave,
Dreams in color, together we believe.
In every challenge, we will stand,
Side by side, hand in hand.

Through storms that rage and skies that clear,
Each moment shared, I hold dear.
In this union, we find our way,
A convergence of love, come what may.

Drifting in Togetherness

In the quiet of twilight's glow,
We find solace, ebb and flow.
Hearts entwined, a gentle breeze,
Whispered dreams, a moment's ease.

Side by side, we wander free,
Underneath the ancient trees.
Laughter dances with the light,
Filling the world, pure delight.

With each step, a story spun,
Threads of gold, two hearts as one.
Together, we embrace the night,
A tapestry of shared delight.

Hand in hand through fields we roam,
Every path leads us back home.
In this journey, side by side,
Drifting in love, our hearts collide.

As the stars begin to shine,
In our dreams, your hand in mine.
Floating softly, time stands still,
Together always, we fulfill.

Ferns of Shared Paths

Amongst the ferns, our shadows dance,
Rooted deep in love's romance.
In the forest, whispers call,
Together, we can have it all.

Each step taken, side by side,
Nature's grace, our living guide.
Leaves like hearts, they flutter near,
In this embrace, we shed each fear.

Sharing dreams beneath the sky,
On this journey, we learn to fly.
With every turn, a story grows,
In the moment, love only flows.

The sacred ferns, a witness true,
To the bond we've built anew.
Through tangled roots, we carve our way,
In sacred silence, love will stay.

As sunlight fades, the moon will rise,
In its glow, our spirits prize.
In the ferns, forever stay,
Together, come what may.

The Heart's Orchestration

In the melody of soft whispers,
Our hearts play on like sweet sisters.
Each note a bond, each beat a tie,
Together soaring, never shy.

Strings of laughter fill the air,
Harmonies crafted with tender care.
In the silence, we find our song,
Together where we both belong.

Like a symphony, love unfolds,
In every touch, warmth behold.
An orchestra of dreams ignite,
In the canvas of the night.

As melodies weave through time,
We dance together, pure and prime.
The heart's orchestration sings,
In every moment, love takes wing.

Bound by chords that never fray,
In the rhythm, come what may.
With each heartbeat, we create,
A future bright, a love innate.

Echoes of Together

In quiet moments, echoes stay,
Reminders of love's gentle sway.
In the distance, soft refrains,
Binding us through joys and pains.

Each laugh a ripple, pure and clear,
Through the silence, I feel you near.
Footsteps echo through the years,
A symphony of shared cheers.

In the whispers of the night,
Together we find our light.
With every heartbeat, stories blend,
In the echoes, love won't end.

Across the valleys, we will roam,
In each echo, we find home.
Through the alleys of our dreams,
Together floating on moonbeams.

As the sun sets on our way,
Echoes will forever stay.
In each moment, through and through,
I hear the echoes, and I'm with you.

The Bridge of Understanding

A silent bridge spans the divide,
Where hearts once whispered, now collide.
In shared gazes, truth is found,
Each step taken, love unbound.

Words like lanterns in the night,
Guide the lost toward the light.
In understanding, we find grace,
Together, we create our space.

Through storms and calm, we weathered time,
Building strength in every rhyme.
With arms extended, we embrace,
Crafting peace in our shared place.

No more walls of fear and doubt,
Just open hearts, and voices shout.
On this bridge, all wounds will mend,
A path where love will never end.

Tides of Intertwined Souls

In the ebb and flow of time,
Two souls dance, a rhythm sublime.
Waves crash softly, hearts entwine,
Bound by fate, our lives align.

Through stormy seas and tranquil skies,
Together we rise, together we sigh.
With every tide, our spirits soar,
Navigating dreams on distant shore.

Secrets whispered with gentle grace,
In the ocean's heart, we find our place.
As stars gaze down, we drift and glide,
In the depths of love, we confide.

Hand in hand, we brave the night,
Guided by the moon's soft light.
Our souls, like currents, will always find,
A home in the waves, forever combined.

Cadence of Embraced Dreams

In twilight's glow, our dreams ignite,
Breathe in magic, feel the light.
Together we weave visions bright,
A tapestry of pure delight.

Each heartbeat echoes a soft refrain,
Of whispered hopes and sweet champagne.
With every challenge, we rise anew,
Hand in hand, we'll see it through.

As dawn breaks in hues so rare,
We dance to rhythms beyond compare.
In unison, our spirits hum,
A symphony of what's to come.

With every breath, we claim our fate,
In dreams embraced, we celebrate.
Through shadows cast, we'll bravely roam,
Finding peace, we make it home.

Threads of Unified Purpose

In the fabric of life, we're tightly sewn,
Threads of purpose, together grown.
Each color vibrant, a tale told,
Binding our journey, woven bold.

With every stitch, we find our way,
United hopes in the light of day.
Through trials faced, we strengthen seams,
Creating beauty from our dreams.

In harmony, we work and strive,
Each thread a heartbeat, we're alive.
Together we stand, a force so grand,
With open hearts, we take a stand.

Through challenges vast, we won't retreat,
In unity, our purpose sweet.
With strength in numbers, we will rise,
A tapestry beneath the skies.

The Flow of Unity

In gentle streams where waters meet,
All hearts converge, their pulses greet.
Dancing rhythms, soft and light,
Together crafting endless night.

Each whisper shared, a bond defined,
In unity, our souls entwined.
Through laughter's grace and sorrow's tears,
We rise as one, dispelling fears.

Branches sway in nature's hand,
Roots entwined beneath the land.
From differences, we weave our song,
In harmony, we all belong.

The stars align, their voices blend,
In cosmic dance, our paths extend.
A tapestry of dreams unfurled,
Together, we embrace the world.

In every moment, grace flows free,
A symphony of you and me.
Through every storm, we'll hold steadfast,
In unity, our bond will last.

Interwoven Destinies

Threads of fate in colors bright,
Weaving stories 'neath the light.
Paths converge, then intertwine,
Destinies marked, a grand design.

With every choice, a strand is drawn,
In silent nights and rosy dawns.
Together we chase, together we fall,
In this dance, we hear the call.

Woven tales of joy and pain,
Through every tear, love's gentle strain.
In shadows deep, we find our way,
Our woven paths, a guiding ray.

Moments shared, a sacred space,
Along this thread, we find our grace.
In the fabric of life, so divine,
Each stitch reflects our hearts align.

Interwoven in every heart,
A journey long that won't depart.
Together we'll write this tale anew,
Bound by the threads of me and you.

The Intimacy of Thoughts

In whispers soft, our minds collide,
A world unseen, we feel inside.
Thoughts like petals, fresh and pure,
In silence shared, we both endure.

What dreams reside in shadowed space,
A sanctuary, our hidden place.
Through quiet glances, secrets spill,
An unspoken bond that time can't kill.

Each notion touches, breaching walls,
In realms where understanding calls.
Intimacy blooms in tender light,
As spirits dance in silent flight.

In every pause, the breath of life,
We delve deeper, without strife.
In this realm of thought and trust,
Our hearts ignite, in love we must.

Together we wander, thought by thought,
In this quiet space, we're gently caught.
The intimacy we hold so dear,
In every thought, we draw you near.

Connective Threads

Threads of gold, stretching far,
Linking hearts, beneath the star.
With every touch, a spark ignites,
In tangled paths, our love ignites.

With gentle hands, we weave our fate,
In every twist, we celebrate.
Through struggles faced and joys embraced,
The threads connect, no time displaced.

Like spider silk in morning's sheen,
Delicate yet strong, unseen.
In every heartbeat, softly said,
These threads of life, forever tied.

Each bond we forge, a sacred thread,
With every word, new paths are spread.
Together, we create our art,
With every stitch, we share our heart.

Connective threads, so tightly spun,
In every soul, our battles won.
With love as glue, we'll never part,
These threads remain within our heart.

Dance of Kindred Spirits

In twilight's embrace, we glide and sway,
With laughter and joy, we light the way.
Each twirl and spin, our hearts entwined,
In this sacred dance, our souls aligned.

Whispers of dreams, like softest breeze,
Carried on winds, they come with ease.
Together we soar, on hope's delight,
In unity's rhythm, we shine so bright.

The moon oversees, a watchful guide,
As we lose ourselves, in love's sweet tide.
With every heartbeat, our spirits rise,
In this dance of life, we claim the skies.

Through time we weave, a tapestry fine,
In the fabric of love, our hearts align.
Together we sing, a melodious chord,
In each other's arms, we are restored.

So let us dance, till the stars appear,
In the magic of now, I hold you near.
For in this moment, forever stays,
Our dance of kindred spirits, ablaze.

The Pulse of Togetherness

In the hush of dawn, we find our way,
With hearts that beat in pure display.
Every glance shared, a silent vow,
Together we flourish, here and now.

In laughter's echo, we find our song,
Each note a bond that keeps us strong.
Through stormy skies and golden light,
In togetherness, we banish the night.

The rhythm of life, in sync we flow,
With hands entwined, our spirits glow.
Every step forward, a journey shared,
In love's embrace, we are prepared.

From valleys low to mountains high,
With whispers of love, we'll touch the sky.
In each heartbeat, the truth we see,
The pulse of togetherness, you and me.

So through the years, let's boldly tread,
With trust and faith, where dreams are spread.
In this life's dance, forevermore,
Our hearts will pulse, a timeless score.

Unveiling the Soul's Symphony

In quiet moments, a melody stirs,
Each note a whisper, where silence blurs.
The heart takes flight, in harmony's grace,
A symphony blooms in this sacred space.

Through trials faced, we find our tune,
In shadows cast by the silver moon.
With every heartbeat, our spirits compose,
An opus of love, where understanding grows.

Strings of the heart, with passion they play,
In rhythms of life, they gently sway.
Together we rise, like a soaring breeze,
In the unveiling, we find our peace.

Every crescendo, a promise to keep,
In the depths of night, where secrets seep.
The symphony echoes through time and space,
As souls intertwine in love's embrace.

So let the music forever resound,
In the hearts of those, where love is found.
In each gentle note, a story unfolds,
Unveiling the soul's symphony, pure gold.

Resonance of Affections

In the garden of dreams, where feelings bloom,
The fragrance of love dispels all gloom.
In gentle whispers, our hearts collide,
Resonance of affections, we can't hide.

Through every smile, a message clear,
In the dance of warmth, we draw near.
With hands that linger, and eyes that gleam,
In this sacred bond, we fiercely dream.

Eager hearts forge a path anew,
With laughter as armor, and love's sweet dew.
Each promise made, a treasure to keep,
In the resonance of affections, love runs deep.

As seasons change, so do we grow,
With roots entangled, our pulse in flow.
In every heartbeat, a story told,
Of resonance so rich, in warmth enfold.

So let us cherish this vibrant place,
Where love's resonance finds its grace.
In the garden of life, our spirits play,
In the resonance of affections, we'll stay.

Vows in the Quiet

In whispers soft beneath the stars,
We thread our dreams in silver bars.
A pact made sweet, no grand display,
In silence, love finds its way.

With every breath, the world stands still,
Two souls entwined, a shared will.
Promises bloom in evening's light,
Our hearts collide in pure delight.

Each moment held, a treasure stored,
In shadows cast, our spirits soared.
Beneath the moon, we mark our place,
In quiet vows, we find our grace.

Hand in hand, we walk so slow,
In whispered tones, our feelings grow.
Forever etched in silent night,
Our love, a guiding star, so bright.

So here we stand, in tranquil pause,
Defining love without a cause.
In every sigh, our hearts repeat,
Vows in the quiet, bittersweet.

The Harmony of Hearts

In every glance, a rhythm flows,
Two beating hearts, a song that grows.
With softest notes, we weave a tune,
A melody under the watchful moon.

Our laughter dances in the air,
With every pulse, we lay our care.
The harmony of souls combined,
In symphonies, our love defined.

Through stormy nights and radiant days,
Together we find the brightest ways.
Our spirits blend, a perfect sound,
In union lost, yet ever found.

In silent moments, chords align,
Each whisper sweet, a sacred sign.
From heart to heart, our music plays,
In every breath, love's gentle praise.

So let the world fade far away,
In our embrace, we choose to stay.
A rhythm born from timeless start,
In every note, the harmony of hearts.

The Forks of Fate

At the crossroads where destinies meet,
Two paths diverge with tender feet.
In every choice, a story unfolds,
In gentle whispers, the future holds.

The winds of change blow soft and sweet,
Guiding our steps with an unseen beat.
With every turn, new dreams ignite,
In the dance of fate, we find our light.

With every fork, a lesson learned,
In every heart, a fire burned.
Through trials faced and joys embraced,
We carve our names where time is paced.

With hands entwined, we face the dawn,
Knowing together, we are reborn.
At every junction, love will guide,
With open hearts, we take the ride.

So here we stand, no fear in sight,
Embracing all that feels so right.
In the tapestry of dreams we create,
We find our way through the forks of fate.

Love's Gentle Alignment

In tender moments, our worlds align,
Two paths converge, a love divine.
With softest glances and quiet sighs,
A bond that blooms beneath the skies.

As stars above find their perfect dance,
In every heartbeat, we take a chance.
With every touch, the cosmos spins,
In love's embrace, true magic begins.

Through trials faced, we rise anew,
In every challenge, my heart stays true.
A gentle touch upon the soul,
In life's great play, love takes its toll.

With whispers sweet and laughter shared,
In moments brief, I know you cared.
With every dawn and every night,
Our love's alignment feels so right.

So let us walk, hand in hand so tight,
In every shadow, we find the light.
With hearts entwined, a sacred sign,
In love's gentle alignment, we brightly shine.

Milton Keynes UK
Ingram Content Group UK Ltd.
UKHW021127021124
450571UK00005B/67

9 789916 890288